THE ROADS JESUS TRAVELED

Sermons And Object Lessons
For Lent And Easter

BY THOMAS A. PILGRIM

C.S.S Publishing Co., Inc.
Lima, Ohio

Library of Congress Cataloging-in-Publication Data

Pilgrim, Thomas A., 1944-
    The roads Jesus traveled : sermons and object lessons for Lent and Easter / by Thomas A. Pilgrim.
        p.   cm.
    ISBN 1-55673-383-6
        1. Lenten sermons.   2. Holy-Week sermons.   3. Easter—Sermons.
4. Sermons, American.   5. Children's sermons.   I. Title.
BV4277.P553   1992
252'.62—dc20
                                                                    91-16969
                                                                    CIP

9201 / ISBN 1-55673-383-6

Dedicated to

my mother
Mrs. Hattie D. Pilgrim

and my wife's mother
Mrs. Irma G. Perryman

Preface

Charles Kuralt has become famous for his CBS News segment, "On The Road With Charles Kuralt." His purpose in those stories is to help us understand ourselves. I have always enjoyed watching them. During one of them I realized it would be possible to preach a series of sermons on the theme, "On The Road With Jesus Christ."

It is in those scenes along the road that we come to understand who Jesus is and what he did. We see him at his best in those places out there on the road.

The season of Lent is itself a journey. It is a journey along the road to the cross and resurrection. One of the things we need to do during Lent is to follow Jesus on the roads he traveled.

It is for this reason that I preached the sermons contained in this book and now offer them to a wider audience. As you read these words, you will understand that out there on the road you travel you will meet another who is with you. In that is the only real self-understanding.

I want to thank my congregation for their response to these messages and my wife Shirley for her continuing encouragement.

Thomas A. Pilgrim

Table Of Contents

The Road To The Wilderness

The Road To The Wilderness

I have always enjoyed that CBS News segment, "On The Road With Charles Kuralt." He takes us to out-of-the-way places like Bethlehem, Georgia; Farmington, Iowa; and Old Town, Maine. He shows us a piece of Americana, and helps us understand ourselves.

So, on the Sundays between now and Easter I want us to go on the road with Jesus of Nazareth — be on the roads Jesus traveled in order that we would see him more clearly and understand more nearly what it is we are to do.

The first road I want us to travel is the road to the wilderness. William Barclay, that great Bible scholar, said that when John the Baptist summoned people to the Jordan river Jesus went there also because he "knew that for him the hour had struck."

Something happened in the mind of Jesus that enabled him to know that now was the appointed time. Something stirred him in such a way that he knew it was time to begin.

And so, one day — with no apparent warning — he walked down that street in Nazareth that led out the south end of town. He took that road that headed down toward Jerusalem, and somewhere along that road he turned eastward toward the Jordan River.

When he arrived at the river he found cousin John the Baptist holding a revival meeting. And Jesus was baptized there, identifying himself with all the people as a sign of God's kingdom and its new age. And, a voice from heaven said, "Thou art my beloved son; with thee I am well pleased." Then Mark writes, "The spirit immediately drove him out into the wilderness." He stayed there for a period of 40 days.

He took the road to the wilderness — because God led him to that place.

11

He took the road to the wilderness — because he needed that time alone to think about what lay ahead.

He took the road to the wilderness — because he needed to prepare for the mission upon which he was about to embark.

He took the road to the wilderness — because he was on a journey from which there was no turning back.

It was a time of personal struggle, trial and testing, not unlike that night he spent in the garden. Jesus spent 40 days in agonizing thought.

Have you ever had a time like that when you were faced with some great decision, and you found yourself torn in many directions? I suspect that many of us have wilderness times when we go down that road to the wilderness and find ourselves truly alone in the midst of some life-changing decision.

Maybe as we look at Jesus in the wilderness we can come to better understand how we can face our own wilderness moments. Look at these things about Jesus on the road to the wilderness.

I

It was a time when Jesus sorted out what he would do. That was one thing he was struggling with. He knew who he was, and what he was all about. He knew what he had to do. But, during that time in the wilderness he clarified his mission, his message and his method.

His mission was to usher in the new age of God's kingdom, to claim the world for God and to offer his own life as proof of God's love. His message was about the kingdom of God, and life in this kingdom — a radical upside down view of the world — entirely different from what people thought. His method was to gather about himself a small group of disciples, train them to spread the message about the mission and to become a redemptive fellowship, his church. Jesus thought about those matters in his wilderness time. He sorted out what he would do.

Do you know what it is you are going to do? I know a man who at the age of 45 was still trying to decide what he was going to do when he grew up. It is about time to get on with it.

Have you decided? What is the direction of your life? And, if you were to arrive at the place where your life is headed now would you be glad to be there?

What are you going to do with life? Is your life best described by the words "getting, grasping, hoarding" — or by the words "giving, loving, sharing?" And, have you decided to follow Jesus on that road he travels — to be a part of his mission — and believe his message — and enlist in his method?

One little boy said in Sunday school, "I want to follow Jesus and spend my entire life serving him. If I can't do that then I want a VCR and a color television."

I heard about a Baptist church which was going to build a new Sunday school building. In an attempt to help raise the money the preacher wired the seats. On the following Sunday at the end of the service he said, "Now, who will give $100 for the building?" He pushed a button and 20 people jumped up. Then he said, "Who will give $500?" He pushed another button and 16 people jumped up. He had a special wire going to where the deacons were seated. He said, "Who will give $1,000?" He pushed that button and 18 deacons were electrocuted. They just would not decide.

Have you sorted out what you are going to do with your life? Could you say in the words of that hymn, "I have decided to follow Jesus, no turning back."

Then, look at something else about Jesus on the road to the wilderness.

II

It was a time when Jesus faced the temptation to be less than he was. That was another thing Jesus did.

Mark does not give us all the details about the temptations of Jesus in the way Matthew and Luke have recorded them.

13

He merely writes in his brief, swiftly moving style, "He was in the wilderness 40 days tempted by Satan."

It is from those other gospels that we learn what those temptations were. They tell us Satan tempted Jesus to use his power in the wrong way, for selfish reasons, to gain an easy victory, an easy following — "Turn these stones into bread — cast yourself off the temple — bow down before me and I will give you all the kingdoms of the world." But, Jesus refused all of that. He had heard the voice of God at his baptism, "Thou art my beloved Son, with thee I am well pleased." And Jesus remembered who he was.

Do you remember who you are? You see, what we do is determined by who we are. That is always the key to every moral and ethical question we face. The answer is determined not so much by what we ought to do, but by who we are. When we have heard the voice of God saying, "Thou art my beloved son or daughter, with thee I am well pleased" — then we know what to do. Then we turn away from the temptation to be less than we are and resolve to be true to all we are, children of God.

Do you remember who you are? Someone else may not remember, but you must remember who you are.

I visited at the nursing home one afternoon. Always when I went I would speak to the ladies who were usually seated by the front door. Most of them knew me, but that day one of them did not remember me. I spoke to them as I walked by and this lady said, "Good Lord, who are they bringing in here now?" Even if those around you forget who you are you remember, and be true to all you are. If you remember you are a child of God then why not be true to that, to all you are?

Jimmy Carter wrote that book *Why Not The Best?* He told of being interviewed by Admiral Rickover who was in charge of the Navy's nuclear submarine program. The admiral asked him how he had done at the Naval Academy. Jimmy Carter was proud to say he was 59th in a class of 220. But then the admiral asked if he had done his best. And Jimmy Carter answered: "No sir, I didn't always do my best." And the admiral said, "Why not?"[1]

14

Why not be true to all you are — a child of God. Jesus made that decision and so can you.

Then look at one other thing about Jesus on the road to the wilderness.

III

It was a time when Jesus made the commitment to see it through. That was the final thing Jesus did. He committed himself to seeing it through — to carrying out this mission God the Father had given him.

No wonder then that later on he was able to pray in the garden, "Not my will but thine be done." Jesus did not make that decision in the garden that night. He made it way back over there in the wilderness at the beginning of his ministry. That is when he made the choice and the commitment to see it through.

You can tell all there is to know about a person's life by the kind of commitments that person has made.

The thing that matters is never the size of a checking account — but the depth of our commitment.

The thing that matters is never the way we dress — but how we live what we profess.

The thing that matters is never the kind of reputation — but having a mind of consecration.

The thing that matters is never our style of living — but cultivating the art of giving.

The thing that matters is never our street location — but traveling the road of dedication.

You can tell all there is to know about a person's life by the kind of commitments that person has made.

That great saint of our church Bishop John Owen Smith used to say, "Give the best you have to the highest you know." I wonder if you are willing to do that? Have you made that kind of commitment?

15

Dr. William H. Henson, pastor at Houston First United Methodist Church, wrote a book several years ago called *Solid Living In A Shattered World.* In that book he told a story about Sam Jones, the great Methodist evangelist. One night he closed a service by asking, "If we could compare the kingdom of God to a locomotive, what part would you like to be?" One person said, "Brother Jones, I'd like to be the whistle and sound God's praises." Another said, "I'd like to be the wheel and just roll down the track." Sam Jones was not really impressed by any of that. But, then one man said, "Brother Jones, I'd like to be the black coal and burn for Christ's sake!" And Sam Jones replied, "Brothers and sisters, we have enough whistles and wheels in the church now. We need more coal."[2]

No church ever moves forward if it is made up of whistles and wheels. Somebody has to be willing to burn for Jesus. What about it? Have you been traveling in the wilderness lately? Have you been trying to figure life out and answer all the questions? Have you been trying to make some big decision about life?

When you come to understand that all the answers are found in him who is the hope of the world then you will be ready to move on out of the wilderness. And you will forever hear the voice of God ringing in your ears, "Thou art my beloved son, my beloved daughter; with thee I am well pleased."

---

1. Carter, Jimmy, *Why Not The Best?*, Broadman Press, Nashville, 1975, p. 8.

2. Henson, William H., *Solid Living In A Shattered World,* Abingdon Press, Nashville, 1985, p. 96.

Pastoral Prayer

Our Father, greater than all our thoughts of thee, whose great hands have reached out beyond the limits of a limitless universe to become a part of our own experience through the coming of thy Son into the world, and who lives within us even now, so touch our hearts and minds in this moment that we would know thee and be able to worship thee.

In this season of Lent as we begin to think of our Lord Jesus turning his face toward Jerusalem, help us to prepare ourselves to journey with him along those roads which led him there. And as we think together of him on those roads may we come to realize that he travels with us on the roads we travel.

Accept our thanksgiving for all thy blessings upon us, for thou art truly the source of life and everything which makes life worthwhile.

Even as we thank thee Father for blessings already given we are bold to ask for other blessings. Give us the blessing of being led by thy Spirit. Give us the blessing of tasks which are greater than our ability. Give us crosses too heavy for us to bear on our own. And on the road too difficult to travel, the mountain too hard to climb, enable us to know our need of thee, so that we would depend upon thee.

Forgive our sins for they are many.

Bless those of our church family and community who need thy help in special ways — those who are sick, or in sorrow, or who have lost their way.

Bless suffering people the world over, for the world is filled with trouble. But thou art the answer to every need, for we have learned it in thy Son, Jesus, in whose name we pray. Amen.

Discussion Questions

Read Aloud: Mark 1:9-13

1. How did Jesus face the decisions he had to make?

2. What factors would you say influenced his thinking?

3. How did Jesus face the temptations? What does this say to us about how we face temptation?

4. What is involved in being true to who we are as God's children?

5. What have you been led to do because of your commitment to Christ and the kingdom of God?

6. Are there times when this commitment has caused difficulty for you? What are the joys you have experienced?

7. What is the most important thing you have learned during your own wilderness times?

Closing: Have one person lead in a time of prayer centered around the thoughts which have been shared.

Better Than A Road Map

Object: A road map

Good morning boys and girls. I am glad that all of you have come to church today. This is a special day in the life of our church. Today is the first Sunday in the season of Lent. Lent is a period of 40 days leading up to Easter Sunday. It is a time when we prepare ourselves to celebrate the victory of Jesus over death. In our talks together we will be thinking about some of the things which happened to Jesus on his way to Jerusalem. I will be speaking in my sermons about the people Jesus met on the roads he traveled. And as I talk with you we will be thinking along these lines.

Who can tell me what this is? That is right, it is a road map. If you are going on a journey you need some way of knowing how to get there, don't you?

One time I was going to see a church member who lived out in the country. I asked someone for directions to that man's house. He said, "You go out of town here and take a left at the first road, go over the bridge and take the first road to the right. Then go down there by a pine tree and take a left. Go over the hill by a corn field and take the second road to the left. Then go to the third road to the right and turn there. You will see a big white house. That's not it. Keep on going until you see a fish pond on the left. There's a brick house just beyond it on the right. That's not it either. You go two miles farther and you will see three houses in a row. I think he lives in one of them."

You know what happened? I never did find that man's house.

The next day another person said to me, "I'll go with you and show you where that man lives." That was much better. That was better than having good directions or road maps. That person went with me.

Jesus went on a journey into the wilderness. He had to find his way. He did find his way with God's help.

We have someone who will travel with us. His help is better than just having a map to follow or some good directions. God will go with each one of us and help us find our way. I want you to always remember that. I'm real glad you were here today.

May we pray: Father, help all of us to find our way. Go with us wherever we travel in life and keep your hands upon us. Amen.

Order Of Worship

Organ Prelude

The Lighting Of The Candles

The Choral Call To Worship

Welcome And Attendance Registration

*The Hymn Of Praise: "Guide Me, O Thou Great Jehovah"

*The Affirmation Of Faith: The Apostles' Creed

*The Gloria Patri

The Children's Message: "Better Than A Road Map"

The Pastoral Prayer

*The Hymn Of Preparation: "O Love Divine, What Hast Thou Done"

*The Dedication Of Tithes And Offerings

The Offertory

*The Doxology

The Anthem

The Message: "The Road To The Wilderness" (Mark 1:9-13)

The Invitation To Christian Discipleship

*The Hymn Of Consecration: "When We Walk With The Lord"

*The Benediction

*The Choral Response

Organ Postlude

*Congregation Standing

The Road To Nazareth

Lent 2
Sermon
Pastoral Prayer
Discussion Questions
Object Lesson
Order of Worship

The Road To Nazareth

Not long ago I was driving down the interstate. I saw standing by the road a young man, not very impressive in appearance, who seemed to have all he owned in two bags. As I went by he held up a sign with one word on it: "Home." I wanted to stop and help him get home and yet because of the way things are today I did not even slow down. But I have often wondered where home was — and if he got there — and what happened when he arrived.

Immediately after his baptism and his time in the wilderness the first thing Jesus did was to head for home, the town of Nazareth.

Oh, you remember Nazareth. It was a two-bit kind of town. It was a town no one really thought much of. It was a town where you would not really want to live. And people often said, "Can anything good come out of Nazareth?" Jesus did. He came out of Nazareth and now he is on his way back — on the road to Nazareth — headed back there at the beginning of his ministry.

I wonder if those people in Nazareth will know him when he gets there? I wonder if they ever really knew him? Who is this Jesus? We have been asking that question, of course, for 2,000 years. We have come up with many good answers, though I suspect that all the answers are less than he is. The sum of the parts is less than Jesus. Who is he?

Is he the Christ of dogma — the Christ of our creeds? Surely those statements tell us who he is. And yet, he is more than the telling of them.

Is he the Christ of the theologically minded, who down through 2,000 years have sought to explain him and have used all their best thinking? Is he the Christ of Saint Augustine, Thomas Aquinas, Karl Barth, Paul Tillich?

Is he the Jesus of history, sought after by those 19th century theologians who knew they could take all the information in the New Testament, put it all together, search out the evidence and come up with a complete biography of Jesus? Is he the one they searched for, only to be challenged by Albert Schweitzer's book, *The Quest of the Historical Jesus*, which said we cannot find out all the details of his life?

Is he the Christ of literature, art and music whose life more than any other person in history has captured the minds of writers, artists and musicians?

Is he the Jesus of revolutionaries, who in every part of the world have found in him their inspiration to create a new order of things?

Is he the Christ of heresies, as old as the church itself, which we still have with us today and which say he is either only a man and nothing more, or completely God and nothing less?

Is he the Jesus of the hippies, Lord of the yuppies, Master of the elite or Savior of the poor?

Is he the Christ of the liberals, the conservatives, the fundamentalists, the charismatics, the right wing or the left or us modern folk in between, or some new version of all of that which has not even been thought up yet?

Who is this Jesus? One thing for sure and for certain, he still remains. Even though he has been scandalized, theologized, apologized, scrutinized and theorized, he still remains. Even though there has been cultural upheaval, political revolution, social evolution and moral pollution, he still remains.

Who is this Jesus? "Is not this Joseph's son?" That was the question they asked that day when he went back home to Nazareth and stood up in church with all the people in his home synagogue and read from the book of Isaiah: "The spirit of the Lord is upon me, because he has anointed me to preach good news to the poor. He has sent me to proclaim release to the captives and recovery of sight to the blind, to set at liberty those who are oppressed, to proclaim the acceptable year of the Lord."

Then he looked at all the home-folks, those with whom he had been raised and he said to them, "Today this Scripture has been fulfilled in your hearing."

How proud they were of him at first. They spoke well of him and wondered at those gracious words, "Is not this Joseph's son? We know him. What a fine young man." But Jesus knew the people at home. And he said, "Doubtless, you will quote to me this proverb, 'Physician, heal yourself.' . . . Truly, I say to you no prophet is acceptable in his own country."

After Jesus had spoken, the home-folks took Jesus out to the edge of town and were going to throw him off the side of a hill because they really did not know who he was.

Who is this Jesus? That is life's ultimate question. Upon the answer rests the answers to all of our questions about the meaning of life. Let me give you some answers which are so simple, yet they contain the most profound truths.

I

He comes to us as one of us. That is who he is. He is the one who comes to us as one of us. When Jesus went back to Nazareth he was one of them, a Nazareth boy. They knew him as one of them.

God sent him to be that. He is God's son, and in a way we can never adequately explain he is God's son in human flesh — the God-Man " . . . who though he was in the form of God, did not count equality with God a thing to be held onto, but emptied himself, taking the form of a servant, being born in the likeness of men."

That is the way Paul put it. He emptied himself of that which was divine and became one of us.

In doing this, he identified himself with all of us. He took upon himself all the pain, sorrow, sin and heartache of those he walked among. He even chose a road that led to death by crucifixion — the ultimate identification with us. In doing this, he comes to us as one of us and takes upon himself all our pain, sorrow, sin and heartache.

The phone rang in the office one morning and a little voice said, "Sorry, this is the wrong number." He hung up before I could say anything, but I wanted to say, "No wait! I'm the wrong number, not you." Jesus came to be one of us, to become the wrong number so that we would have the right number.

I read somewhere about a young man in college who had a placement one quarter for a few hours a week in a nursing home. His first day he confessed to his supervisor he did not know what to say. The supervisor said, "Good, you see that lady over there. Go over and say hello." He walked over and said, "Hello." She asked, "Are you a relative?" He answered, "No." She said, "Good! I hate my relatives! Sit down!"

Jesus is a relative of ours who has come to us — Son of God and our brother — who makes us become the children of God also. He comes to us as one of us.

II

He comes to us where we are. That is also who he is. He is the one who comes to us where we are. He went home to his own people first and met them where they were. He knew where they were. And he knew also that "No prophet is acceptable in his own country." But even so he went to them.

You see this throughout the New Testament accounts of his life. Wherever people were, that is where he went. He went to a wedding feast — and out around the lake — and up on the side of a hill — and along a dusty road — and in the middle of town — and into all those homes — wherever there were people who had troubles, problems, pains, sins and sorrows, he went to them.

Because he met them where they were he had a way of putting them at ease. Sometime people are really uncomfortable around preachers and they have this overwhelming compulsion to demonstrate their ignorance of the Bible. Once on "The Jeffersons" the preacher came to see George. In response to some statement made by the preacher George said, "Well, it's like the Bible says, it is easier for a needle to get into heaven than it is for a rich man to get in a camel's eye." But no one was very uptight around Jesus. He put them at ease where they were and because of that he was able to call out the best from them.

Where are you right now? A teacher asked her fifth grade students how many points there are on a compass. One boy said, "Five!" She said, "No, there are four." He replied, "But I can prove it. There is north, south, east, west and the place where I am right now."

Wherever you are right now Jesus is the one who comes to you and he can put your life at ease. He will make himself a part of your struggle. He will say the right thing — the healing word, the hopeful word, the forgiving word, the helpful word, the lifting word — and he will call out the best from within you. He comes to us where we are.

III

He comes to us and calls us to go with him. That is also who he is. He is the one who calls us to go with him. Jesus left Nazareth and went on the road. No one from Nazareth went with him. He called no disciples from Nazareth and no one volunteered. But he does call us to go with him — and out on other roads. For whoever we are and whatever we are, he does not leave us as we are. He calls us to become more than we are and to move on further than we are. He says to us as he said to those fishermen by the lake in the long ago, "Follow me and I will make you become fishers of men."

A preacher was working on two sermons for the coming Sunday. Being the month of June one had to do with a graduation theme and for Sunday night something else. Late Friday evening he received a call saying the graduation speaker at a nearby girls college was ill and could he fill in at the last minute? He said he would and asked his wife to put his sermon in his Bible and give it to him as he went out the door. He arrived a few minutes late, just in time to speak. He walked over to the podium, opened his Bible and read out the first line — not knowing his wife had picked up the wrong sermon — "Follow me and I will make you fishers of men." That was good news for those girls.

The good news is that Jesus calls us to come and go with him, to follow him, to become servants, fishers and followers, witnesses, to become more than we are.

Dr. Maxie Dunnam, a United Methodist minister in Memphis, Tennessee, wrote a book called *Jesus' Claims — Our Promises*. He told the story of Washington Gladden, a minister who lived back at the turn of the century. As a young man he had sought to know Christ, but was not able to find the peace he was told he should have. He attended services, read, prayed and followed all kinds of suggestions. But he could never find the experience others had. Then one day he met a minister who understood what he was going through. He told the young man to walk in the ways of Christ and serve him, and to trust God whether he felt right or not. That was the thing he needed to hear. He began to follow Christ in all he did. He gave his life in service and became a minister. And he sought to relate the Christian gospel to the problems of his time. He was one of the leaders of the church in this country. His commitment to Christ was expressed in these words: "O Master, let me walk with thee in lowly paths of service free; Tell me thy secret; help me bear the strain of toil, the fret of care. Help me the slow of heart to move by some clear winning word of love; Teach me the wayward feet to stay, and guide them in the homeward way."[1]

Who is this Jesus? He is the one who comes to us and calls us to go with him — to walk with him. Unless you come to grips with who this Jesus is you will never know who you are, and what your life is all about.

---

1. Dunnam, Maxie, *Jesus' Claims — Our Promises,* The Upper Room, Nashville, Tennessee, 1985, p. 55.

Pastoral Prayer

O God, our Father, we bow before thee today because we have come to know that all our hopes and dreams are bound up in thy will, thou who art the source of all good things. So, be near us in this time of worship and may our songs of praise bring glory to thy name.

We are mindful today, O God, of the journey of our Lord on the roads he traveled. Keep us ever mindful of him during these days of Lent.

We thank thee, gracious Father, for all the ways our lives are blessed of thee. We have seen thy hand at work in our lives, and we know that out of thy goodness all good gifts have been showered upon us. Accept our thanksgiving and help us to have thankful lifestyles — lives which are the expression of thy goodness toward us and our willingness to be a blessing so that other lives may be blessed of thee.

Forgive our sins, merciful Father, and restore to us the joy of thy salvation. Turn on the light of love in our hearts that they would be strangely warmed and may the light of that love shine in us and through us that we would be a light which shines in the darkness even as our Lord Jesus was the light of the world and calls us to be the light in a world threatened by darkness.

Be near our sick. Comfort those who mourn. Guide those who lose their way. Touch those who despair. And we will give thee honor and glory, through Jesus Christ, our Lord. Amen.

Discussion Questions

Read Aloud: Luke 4:16-30

1. Who do you think Jesus is?

2. What is there about Jesus that touches your life the most?

3. In what ways have you found in Jesus, his message, his ministry and his mission, liberation, help and hope?

4. In what ways do you feel Jesus has identified himself with you? How do you identify yourself with him?

5. How do you think Jesus and the Christian gospel speak to you where you are?

6. In what ways do you feel the call of God in your life?

7. How does following Jesus help you know who you are?

Closing: Have a time of sentence prayers to be ended by the group leader.

God's Calling Card

Object: A calling card

Good morning boys and girls. I want you to know I am so glad that you are here today. This Sunday morning we are thinking about a Scripture lesson that tells us about Jesus going back to his home town of Nazareth. Jesus grew up there in that town. And at the beginning of his ministry he decided that he would go back there and preach to the people in his own home church or synagogue. One of the things we will be thinking about today is the fact that Jesus still comes to be with us whoever we are and wherever we are.

Who can tell us what this is? Okay, it is a card and this is a special kind. It is a "calling card." This has the name of our church on it and my name. I can go see some person and if they are not at home I can leave this in their door and they will know that I have been there.

If I go to visit someone who is in the hospital and that person is not in his or her room, I can leave this and they will know I have been there to see them. I can also write them a message on this card like, "Sorry I missed you," or "Hope you feel better" or "I am praying for you."

In a way we could say God has a calling card he has left with us. His Son Jesus brought it into the world. And it has a message for us. The message is, "God so loved the world that he gave his only son that whoever believes in him should not perish but have everlasting life."

There are a lot of ways we get that message. We find it in the Bible as we study and learn in Sunday school. We learn from other people that God loves us as we share his love with each other. We get the message in all the ways God has blessed us and all the good things God does for us.

33

Now I am going to give each one of you one of these calling cards. It has our church's name on this side and mine. And on the back it has a message from me to you that I have written. And the message says, "I love you!"

Thank you for being here with us today.

May we pray: Father, thank you for loving each one of us and making us to be your children. And thank you for sending us the message. Amen.

Order Of Worship

Organ Prelude

The Lighting Of The Candles

The Choral Call To Worship

Welcome And Attendance Registration

*The Hymn Of Praise: "All Hail The Power Of Jesus' Name"

*The Affirmation Of Faith: The Apostles' Creed

*The Gloria Patri

The Children's Message: "God's Calling Card"

The Pastoral Prayer

*The Hymn Of Preparation: "Jesus, I My Cross Have Taken"

*The Dedication Of Tithes And Offerings

The Offertory

*The Doxology

The Anthem

The Message: "The Road To Nazareth" (Luke 4:16-30)

The Invitation To Christian Discipleship

*The Hymn Of Consecration: "More Love To Thee, O Christ"

*The Benediction

*The Choral Response

Organ Postlude

*Congregation Standing

The Road To Capernaum

Lent 3
Sermon
Pastoral Prayer
Discussion Questions
Object Lesson
Order of Worship

Sermon For Lent 3
Mark 1:21-28

The Road To Capernaum

Dr. Robert V. Ozment served for many years as the pastor of the First United Methodist Church in Atlanta, Georgia. In one of his books, *Love Is The Answer*, he told about a lady he went to see in the hospital. She was very complimentary in the things she said about him. She said, "You are the best preacher I have ever heard. I've read some of your books, and you are a great author. You are the sweetest, kindest person in the world. You are a very handsome man." Just then her nurse came in and he started to leave. She walked over to the door and said, "Dr. Ozment, I don't know what she might have told you, but she is losing her mind, so don't believe anything she said." And, Bob Ozment replied, "She carried on a perfectly grand conversation, and I believe every word she said."[1]

I do not know of anyone who has more kind things said about them than preachers. We receive far more compliments than we deserve. Most people just naturally love their preacher and will bend over backward to say something nice.

I know there have been many times during my ministry when I have not done a very good job on Sunday morning. But I do not ever remember any person ever coming out the door and saying to me, "Well, preacher today you were lousy." I have gone home feeling that way at times, but no one has ever said that to me.

I did have one member who used to say, "Preacher, that was a warm sermon you preached today." I would always thank him for that. It made me feel good. But, one day he told me, "A warm sermon is one that is not so hot!"

When Jesus left Nazareth where he had not been well received, he went on the road for a three-year tour of preaching, teaching, healing, helping, judging, forgiving, enabling, challenging, calling and lifting. He was well received in most places — for a while. "The common people heard him gladly."

Mark tells us that in those early days of his ministry he was in the area of the Sea of Galilee. There he called Andrew, Simon, James and John to be disciples. Then they went into town there on the northern shore of the lake. The name of the town was Capernaum.

While there in Capernaum Jesus taught in the synagogue and astonished all who heard him with the things he said and did. That evening they went to the home of Simon where Jesus stayed while in Capernaum. As we look at the events which took place in that little town we get a glimpse of how Jesus carried out his entire ministry. I think we see there also the impact he makes upon our lives. Think about these things.

I

Jesus taught people from a higher level of authority. No one had ever heard words like those Jesus spoke. When Jesus and his new disciples went into Capernaum they went to the synagogue where he taught. Those who heard him were astonished at his teaching, for "he taught as one who had authority and not as the scribes."

No one had taught like this before. It was a new teaching above the Law and the prophets. It was the fulfillment of them both. The people had been hearing the Scripture read in the synagogue for a long time. They had heard all the commentaries. They knew the Scriptures backward and forward, from cover to cover. But Jesus brought them a new message for he personified what he said. He was the fulfillment of all that had gone before. He was the incarnation of God's Word. In him the word was made flesh.

That is always in every age one of the great needs of the church. We must find a way to personify what we believe.

We must let the written word live in us. For you see, it does no good to know the word — unless you let the word live. You can know the Bible backward and forward, but unless you live it — unless you allow it to become incarnational — it does no good.

Henry David Thoreau said of the New Testament, "Most people favor it outwardly, defend it with bigotry and hardly ever read it." Even if we read it, that is not enough. We have to live it.

I have a Bible collection which contains many different translations, versions and languages, 55 in all. I have 55 Bibles. But the most important thing is to live by just one of them.

I once rode past a little church with a big sign out front advertising a singing on Saturday night. But the wind had blown off one of the letters and the sign read, "Gospel Sin ing Saturday Night." I bet they drew a crowd. There is a lot of gospel sinning that goes on — people talking about the gospel, but never getting around to living it.

Years ago I said two things in a sermon one Sunday which one person really took seriously. One thing I said was, "Live — don't just exist." The other thing was, "Lift — don't lean." One of the young women in our church was struck by that. She wrote down those two ideas on her tennis shoes, one on the right and one on the left. She took those two thoughts home with her and she wore them to school the next week.

What might happen in your life and in the life of the church if we allowed the word to be written upon our hearts, if we allowed it to be incarnational? Then think about something else.

II

Jesus touched people with a higher level of compassion. No one had ever seen the things Jesus did. While teaching in the synagogue that day Jesus healed a man who had an unclean spirit. The people were amazed at what they saw. They said, "What is this? A new teaching! With authority he commands even the unclean spirits and they obey them." It was a new teaching which produced compassionate action.

No one had ever shown this kind of compassion. He healed the sick, all who were brought to him. He did it not to attract attention, or to gain a reputation, or to make money or to have his own television show. He did it for one reason. He was moved with compassion.

Jesus touched people with a higher level of compassion. And in that he demonstrated the love of God. That is another thing he calls us to do. He calls us to cultivate in our lives this higher level of compassion — to demonstrate the love of God.

It does no good for us to talk about the love of God unless that love is a living reality in our lives. Sometimes the things we do demonstrate not the love of God, but the love of self — the love of status — the love of race — the love of class — the love of kith and kin and group. But Jesus always called people away from that to a deeper kind of love — to a higher level of compassion. He gave sight to the blind, food to the hungry, hope to the hopeless, forgiveness to the sinner and encouragement to the downtrodden. He entrusted that kind of ministry to his disciples and told them to do the same things.

That is our calling today — not to be people who talk about religion — who parade a false kind of goodness — but who demonstrate the love of God by reaching out to all God's children with a higher level of compassion.

I remember reading about a girl who lived in an orphanage. One day the lady in charge of her cabin saw her walk out to a fence by the road and place a piece of paper in a knothole in a tree. When the girl went back into her cabin the lady went out to the tree to find out what was on the paper. She took it out of the knothole and read these words, "To whoever finds this, I love you."

God sent his Son with those words written across his life. The Son sent his disciples with those words written across their lives. If you are a disciple then you must have those words written across your life. Then think about this.

III

Jesus took people to a higher level of service. No one had ever been challenged to a level of service like this before. When they left the synagogue that day Jesus and his disciples went to the home of Simon where they would stay. When they arrived they found Simon's wife's mother was sick. Jesus went into her, lifted her up, "and the fever left her; and she served them." No one had ever lifted people to that level of service. When this sick woman was made well she apparently served them a meal. But there is a greater implication here — a little hidden message. Surely Mark knew what he was doing when he wrote it this way. All the people touched by Jesus were lifted to a new level of service, a higher level.

When our lives are touched by Jesus he takes us to a new level of service. Faith always produces good works. The proof is always in the pudding.

A preacher friend of mine went to see a family who had recently visited his church. This couple said, "What does your church have to offer us?" He thought a minute and said, "I would like to know what you have to offer our church." That is always the question isn't it?

It is not what can I get out of church, but what can I put into it. It is not what does the church have to offer me, but what do I have to offer the church. It is not how can the church meet my needs, but what goal does my church need me to meet. It is not how high can you jump, but how straight can you walk. It is not the height of your enthusiasm, but the depth of your commitment.

I remember visiting a family years ago. They had been worshiping in our church for some time, but continued to keep the church at a safe distance. The young wife said, "We have thought about joining the church, but we are waiting for God to give us that good feeling you are supposed to have." I do not know why I did, but I said, "You have a long wait. God is not going to tell you when to join and you will never have that good feeling until you do. The good feeling comes as a result of commitment to Jesus Christ and dedication to his church. Then, and only then.'' They did make that commitment and joined the church. And a couple of Sundays later as they came out of church she said to me, "We have that good feeling now." Their lives had been lifted to a new level of service.

Jesus Christ will lift your life to a new level of service if you will dare let go of whatever it is that holds you back and reach out and take hold of his hand.

_____

1. Ozment, Robert V., *Love Is The Answer*, Fleming H. Revell Company, Old Tappan, New Jersey, 1967, p. 43.

Pastoral Prayer

Almighty God, our Heavenly Father, who has sent thy Son, Jesus Christ, to be the Word of life for us, so touch our hearts that we would be filled with thy love, and know the reality of the Living Word.

In this season, Father, as we think of the journey of our Lord, enable us to travel with him, watch with him, pray with him, that we would know the reality of his presence in the world and in our lives today.

Accept our worship, O God, for we have come to offer thee our adoration, our devotion and our lives. We recognize thee as the source of life, the creator of the universe who has created in us thine own image. We know thou hast called us to be thy people, thy children, brothers and sisters in the family of God. And so we join in worship, service and fellowship together. Bless us as we seek to be thy church.

We offer thee our thanksgiving, O God, for all thy bountiful blessings upon us. For thy goodness we thank thee. For all the gifts of home and church, friends and community, work and play, we thank thee O God.

Continue to bless us, Father, with the vision of what thou would have us do as a church. And give us the leadership of thy spirit.

Bless those of our church family and community who are sick and need the strength which comes from thee. Touch them with thy healing touch.

Bless suffering people the world over and use what we are and have to bless those in need.

We ask all of this in Christ's name. Amen.

Discussion Questions

Read Aloud: Mark 1:21-28

1. What were the main emphases of the ministry of Jesus?

2. What qualities did Jesus bring to his ministry?

3. How do we as Christians today embody these same qualities?

4. What was the authority behind the teaching of Jesus?

5. How do we allow the message of Jesus to be incarnational for us?

6. What does it mean to have compassion? What are some ways we can do this?

7. What new levels of service might be open to you as a result of your commitment to Jesus?

Closing: Center your thinking on ways the ideas shared may be made real and invite several people to pray that this may be accomplished.

The Glue Of God's Love

Object: A bottle of glue

Good morning boys and girls. I am glad you are here. Today in the Scripture lesson we will be reading about Jesus going to a town called Capernaum.

Today I want you to look at this bottle of glue. They call this "School Glue." This is the same kind you use in school. As you already know this is really good glue because you can stick anything together with this glue. You can glue paper, plastic, wood, cloth, and just about anything else you can think of and it will stay together. Another good thing about it is that you cannot glue yourself to the floor. I was using some really strong glue one time and I actually glued myself to the floor. But you will not do that with this glue. Also, this glue will wash off your hands and clothes. So it will not make a mess you cannot clean up. Your mother does not have to worry when you use this glue.

Now, let me ask you this question. Have you ever heard the expression, "I'm stuck on you?" Do you know what that means? It means, "I love you." It is something one of you boys might someday say to one of these girls.

There is a glue in life that joins us together in the church. It helps us stick with our friends and our family members. Who knows what that is?

It is God's love. God's love is like glue. It will hold you together when nothing else will.

Jesus said to his disciples one time, "Children, love one another." He loved each one of them. And he wanted them to love each other.

Everywhere Jesus went he called people to come follow him. And in doing that he was teaching them to have the same love and concern for other people that he had.

Still today he wants us to be people who love him, love God, love each other and love other people, who more than anything, just need someone to love them. I am glad you came here today.

May we pray: O God, help us to love each other and to love you. Help us to share your love with others. Amen.

Order Of Worship

Organ Prelude

The Lighting Of The Candles

The Choral Call To Worship

Welcome And Attendance Registration

*The Hymn Of Praise: "Praise To The Lord, The Almighty"

*The Affirmation Of Faith: The Apostles' Creed

*The Gloria Patri

The Children's Message: "The Glue Of God's Love"

The Pastoral Prayer

*The Hymn Of Preparation: "Tell Me The Stories Of Jesus"

*The Dedication Of Tithes And Offerings

The Offertory

*The Doxology

The Anthem

The Message: "The Road To Capernaum" (Mark 1:21-28)

The Invitation To Christian Discipleship

*The Hymn Of Consecration: "Rise Up, O Men Of God"

*The Benediction

*The Choral Response

Organ Postlude

*Congregation Standing

The Road To Samaria

Lent 4
Sermon
Pastoral Prayer
Discussion Questions
Object Lesson
Order of Worship

The Road To Samaria

When I was growing up we had a joke in our family about my father's shortcuts. Whenever we were off on a trip somewhere he always knew a quicker way to get there, or back home.

I remember one time when I was about 10 years old we were on the way home one night. My father decided to take one of his shortcuts. He made a turn to the left, went around a curve, took the first right, then back to the left, and we wound up in the middle of a cornfield.

At one point in his ministry Jesus was in the area of Judea. He had been there on his preaching, teaching mission and word came to him that the Pharisees were hearing that he was baptizing more people than John the Baptist. The Pharisees were greatly concerned about all the excitement being stirred up. So Jesus decided it would be better if he went back up to the area of Galilee. He chose the road to Samaria.

Most Jews really did not like traveling through Samaria. They would take a long shortcut traveling east, crossing the Jordan River, going around Samaria and coming back into Galilee. The most direct route, however, was to go straight through Samaria.

Jesus was in a hurry to leave Judea. So he went right straight through Samaria. That was the quickest shortcut. The Revised Standard Version reads, "He had to go through Samaria." The King James Version states it, "He must needs go through Samaria."

We do not know how many times Jesus passed through Samaria. But we are struck by the fact that he did, because the Samaritans were looked down upon by the Jews. The Samaritans were looked upon as being "half-breeds." No good

Jew would associate with them. But Jesus went there — "He must needs go through Samaria."

About noon one day they came to Jacob's Well. Jesus was tired from the journey. He sat down there beside the well. And the disciples went on into town, another mile or so up the road, to buy something for lunch. While Jesus was there at the well a woman came to draw water. When Jesus saw her he said, "Give me a drink."

The woman was a little surprised and said, "How is it that you, a Jew, asks a drink from me, a woman of Samaria?" Jesus answered, "If you knew the gift of God, and, who it is that is saying to you, 'Give me a drink,' you would have asked him and he would have given you living water." The woman then replied, "Sir, you have nothing to draw with and the well is deep; where do you get that living water?" Then Jesus said to her, "Everyone who drinks of this water will thirst again, but whoever drinks of the water that I shall give him will never thirst; the water that I shall give him will become in him a spring of water welling up to eternal life." And the woman responds, "Sir, give me this water, that I may not thirst, nor come here to draw."

In this story of Jesus and the woman at the well — on the road through Samaria — we see some very basic things about the meaning of Christian faith.

I

We find the response we need the most. That is one thing here in this story of the woman at the well. She came there looking for a precious resource — something no person could survive without. She came there looking for water. But Jesus offered her living water from a spring which would well up into eternal life. At first she did not know what he meant. She said, "Sir, give me this water, that I may not thirst, nor come here to draw."

As they talked Jesus enabled her to understand the real thirst in her life — the real vacuum there — and how it could be filled up only by worshiping and serving God in spirit and in truth. She said, "I know that Messiah is coming (he who is called Christ); when he comes he will show us all things." Jesus said, "I who speak to you am he." At that moment she found something she had never known before — the one thing she needed the most.

There is one thing we need more than anything else — one resource — and that is a spring of living water which quenches our thirst for meaning in life — for the secret to our existence — and for hope in the present and all the future that awaits us. We need that living water.

That living water — that resource we need — is Christian faith, faith in Jesus Christ, who meets us out on the roads we travel and offers to us a cup of water, living water, water which wells up into life, which gives us life.

There is no other resource for living which will see us through. And there is enough of that water to see us through.

I remember reading years ago about a woman who lived in one of the poorer sections of New York City. She had lived there all her life and had raised her family there. They had always lived in poverty and she had never been able to provide them with enough of anything. She became involved in a community program for the elderly, and one day they went on a trip to the beach. She had never been there before, had never seen the ocean. She stood there on the beach and said, "Look at all that water. For the first time in my life I am able to see something there is enough of."

There is enough living water for all of us. We all need it because no other resource will see us through.

Then there is something else in this story.

II

We find the response we are to make. After we receive the living water there is only one response that is appropriate. It is not enough to say "Thank you" — or, to say "My, this is good water" — or to say "I am so glad I have it" — or to say "Look at me, I've been drinking from the well. Don't you wish you had some?"

There is only one response that is acceptable. This woman at the well left the well and went to find her friends. After Jesus identified himself to her she did not say anything else. John tells us that she left and went into the city and said to all the people, "Come, see a man who told me all that I ever did. Can this be Christ?" And they left the city and went with her. She brought her friends to Christ.

This kind of thing happened in so many places. Have you ever noticed in the gospels how many people found Jesus — or were found by him — and then went to tell someone else about him? Andrew met Jesus. Then he went to find his brother Simon and brought him to meet Jesus. Philip met Jesus. Then he went to find Nathaniel and brought him to Jesus. A wild man lived in a cemetery. He met Jesus. Then he went into town and told everyone he knew about him.

Why do you think those gospel writers recorded these events? Because they wanted all Christians to know that once you meet Jesus you cannot keep it a secret. You simply must go tell someone about it. That is what it means to be a Christian. That is the kind of response we are supposed to make.

I know a man who is a friend of John Stewart, who was a part of the Kingston Trio. John Stewart said to this man, "God speaks to each of us a little differently, hoping we will tell each other." That is the response.

We are called to tell someone in some way, to find someone somehow and share in some way what we know.

A man who lived in a big city became tired of robbers breaking into his apartment. So he started leaving a note on his door, "I may not hear the bell. I am back in the kitchen." He came home from work one day and found his apartment turned upside down. There was a note on the kitchen table, "I looked for you everywhere but could not find you." Go find someone.

I once heard United Methodist minister Dr. Maxie Dunnam speak at an evangelism conference. He said he loved that hymn, "What a Friend We Have In Jesus." But he said he likes to turn it around, "What a Jesus we have in friends." A friend of Jesus helps make other friends for Jesus.

Then there is one other thing in this story.

III

We find the result of our mission. Receiving the living water and responding to it by passing it around always produces a result. Our mission as the people of God produces a result always. When the woman at the well reached town she told everyone about meeting Jesus. John writes that "Many Samaritans from that city believed in him because of the woman's testimony."

Then when they came out to meet Jesus they asked him to stay there with them for a while. Jesus stayed in the town for two days. Those third class people in that second class town gave Jesus first class treatment. Jesus accepted their hospitality. He treated them like first class citizens of the kingdom of God. And John says, "Many more believed because of his Word." Then the people told the woman they no longer believed in him because of what she said, but now they believed in him because they heard his words. What this woman did bore much fruit in the kingdom of God.

When you and I think of the living water and start passing that cup around, some amazing things begin to happen. No longer do other people just take our word that this is good water. They begin to discover on their own for themselves that this is the water of life — living water that wells up into eternal life.

That is why the church is here and that is why the Lord God has called us to be persons who serve him.

Dr. Alan Walker is a world-renowned preacher from Australia. He tells of a man who moved from England to

Sydney, Australia in the year 1810. He gained a grant of land on the Hawkesbury River. There his son John grew up. But John became an alcoholic at an early age. He was greatly troubled by this and was converted at a Methodist revival. He gave his life to God and became a Methodist preacher. He died in his 30s, but his son Aaron took over his preaching circuit at the age of 16. Five of Aaron's sons became Methodist preachers. The son of one of them is Alan Walker, one of the world's most respected church leaders. Alan Walker has a son who is a preacher. In all, there are 14 preachers over five generations in that family.[1] They are all the result of what happened in the life of one man who was drowning in alcohol and dying of thirst. But one person offered him a real drink of real water — living water. Who could ever measure the far-reaching results of that one little sip?

Who knows what might happen if you were to offer living water to someone who is dying of thirst? It just might become in them a well of living water that springs up into eternal life.

Would you give someone else a drink?

---

1. Walker, Alan, *God, The Disturber,* Word Books Publisher, Waco, Texas, 1973, p. 7.

Pastoral Prayer

O God in Heaven, great God and creator of all the universe, who has flung the stars out across an endless sky and counted every grain of sand on every beach, who knows when a tiny sparrow falls to the ground, we thy children gather to worship thee knowing that each of us is worth more to thee than the brightest star.

As we think about thy Son and our Savior moving toward the cross and his date with destiny, fill our minds with a new and deeper understanding of him. May we travel with him down roads of deeper commitment.

We thank thee, O God, for all thy gifts of love and mercy, for thy grace at work in our lives and works of grace which transform our living. We thank thee for hopes that lift and for lifting us from hopeless situations. We thank thee for love that is patient and loving us when we have tried thy patience. We thank thee for thy bountiful goodness and for the bounty we may share because thy goodness has gotten down on the inside of us.

Grant us thy forgiveness, Father, for though we have professed to be thy children we have sought our own way. We have done things our way. We have followed the desires of our hearts. And the world is a mess because of what we have done and not had the courage or the love to do. So forgive us.

Fill our hearts with love, kindness, goodness, pity, selflessness, generosity, hope and faith.

Bless our sick, lonely, distressed, those who are afraid. Give them hope in thee and be the Great Physician for them.

We ask all of this in the name of our Lord Jesus. Amen.

Discussion Questions

Read Aloud: John 4:1-6

1. What did it mean for Jesus to go through Samaria?

2. Do you feel there have been times when you have also gone through Samaria?

3. In what ways can you identify with the woman at the well?

4. What does the term "living water" mean to you? In what ways has this water quenched your own thirst?

5. How are we to respond to this gift of living water? In what ways can we do this?

6. Who are the people around us today who need the gift of living water?

7. How can we better share the good news with these people who need living water?

Closing: Have a time of silent prayer, thinking about the experiences shared. Have one person end with prayer.

Living Water

Object: A canteen

Good morning boys and girls. I am glad that all of you
have come to church today. The Scripture lesson we will be
reading today is the story of the woman at the well.

Who can tell us what this is? It is a canteen. You can carry
water in this canteen if you are out on a hike.

Years ago I was in the army. I remember one day we went
out on a hike of about 15 miles. Fifteen miles is longer than
a hike, isn't it? It was really a long, long walk. It was in the
summer and I remember it was a really hot day. The only water
we had was the water in the canteens. We had to make that
last all day. Before we finished the hike we all ran out of water
and we were really thirsty.

There is a story in the Bible about Jesus being out on a
long walk. He went through an area called Samaria. While
on that journey he and his disciples came to a well. The disciples went on into town to buy some food. But Jesus stayed
there at the well. Soon a woman came there and she and Jesus
had a long talk that day.

Do you remember what they were talking about? That is
right. They were talking about water. This woman thought
Jesus meant the kind of water we drink. But Jesus was talking about a different kind of water. He told this woman he
could give her a kind of water that would keep her from ever
being thirsty again. But he was not talking of the water we
drink. He told her he would give her some living water and
this water would become in her a well that springs up into everlasting life. If she would drink that water she could live forever
in God's kingdom.

Jesus was talking to her about believing in him and being one of his followers. He was saying all we need to be a child of God is to have all that we need and to know how to live.

One time Jesus was preaching to people out on a hill. We call what he said, "The Sermon on the Mount." He said in those words that day, "Blessed are those who hunger and thirst for righteousness for they shall be satisfied." Those people who are thirsty to know God and live for God will find God. Their thirst will be satisfied by the living water Jesus gives us.

I am glad all of you were here today.

May we pray: O God, thank you for your Son Jesus, and the living water he gives all of us. Amen.

Order Of Worship

Organ Prelude

The Lighting Of The Candles

The Choral Call To Worship

Welcome And Attendance Registration

*The Hymn Of Praise: "Ask Ye What Great Thing I Know"

*The Affirmation Of Faith: The Apostles' Creed

*The Gloria Patri

The Children's Message: "Living Water"

The Pastoral Prayer

*The Hymn Of Preparation: "Amazing Grace"

*The Dedication Of Tithes And Offerings

The Offertory

*The Doxology

The Anthem

The Message: "The Road To Samaria" (John 4:1-6)

The Invitation To Christian Discipleship

*The Hymn Of Consecration: "Jesus The Very Thought Of Thee"

*The Benediction

*The Choral Response

Organ Postlude

*Congregation Standing

The Road To Jericho

Lent 5
Sermon
Pastoral Prayer
Discussion Questions
Object Lesson
Order of Worship

The Road To Jericho

What would happen if you lost your sight? In June, 1985 I had surgery for a brain tumor. When the doctor came in my room the first night I was in the hospital, he told me what my prospects were. He said I could lose my sight in one or both eyes, or my speech, or the ability to walk. He said I might not even live through the surgery. So the possibilities were frightening. I remember saying to the doctor, "I only need one good eye. More than that I need to be able to speak." I knew a preacher needed his voice more than he needed his vision. But still I did not want to lose the ability to see. None of us would want to lose our sight. Think how it might have been if you had been born blind — if you had never been able to see.

The roads Jesus chose to follow carried him always closer to Jerusalem. At one point Luke writes in his gospel, "He set his face to go to Jerusalem." He took that turn in the road which would finally lead him there. And on that road he came to Jericho.

As he came down the road to Jericho there was a great crowd of people who were with him. They knew who Jesus was by now and they had all gone out to meet him. As they came near the city limits of Jericho there was a blind man there by the road. Mark, in his gospel, identifies him as Bartimaeus.

The blind man was not able to see but he was aware that something important was happening. He heard the noise of the crowd. He stood up, reached out and grabbed someone by the arm and said, "What is it? What is happening?" They answered, "Jesus of Nazareth is passing by." He may have been blind, but he knew who Jesus was. He had heard all about Jesus. The blind always listen more intently. But he had no idea Jesus would ever come down his road.

67

Immediately he cried out, "Jesus, Son of David, have mercy on me." Those standing there thought he was being rude — getting out of his place. They said, "Pipe down, Bart." But he cried out all the more, "Son of David, have mercy on me!" Jesus looked at him — saw his shabby clothing — his faltering steps — the distant look on his face — Jesus knew he was blind.

What about it? What is it that is hurting you? Have you been living in the dark?

I want you to remember that all of us are Bartimaeus. You think about that blind man on the road, unable to find his way, uncertain about the present and the future. That is us. We are Bartimaeus. That being the case, would you remember these things?

I

Jesus invites you into his presence. Jesus invited the blind man to come to him. Luke tells us that when Jesus heard the cries of the blind man he stopped, "and commanded him to be brought to him." Jesus invited Bartimaeus.

Jesus always invited people to come to him. He said, "Come unto me all who labor and are heavy laden and I will give you rest."

Later, when Jesus got into Jericho he found Zacchaeus up a tree. Jesus said, "Zacchaeus, come down out of that tree, for I must stay at your house today."

That was the invitation Jesus gave people everywhere he went, on every road he traveled, "Come and follow me."

Jesus invites us all to come into his presence — to bring to him who we are and whatever is happening to us. The door to his presence is always open.

A man told his preacher there were always people coming to see him. They had these little satchels they carried, filled with literature they gave out and they tried to convert him to their religion. He never knew what to say. His preacher said,

"I'll tell you what to do. Hang a big American flag over your fireplace, invite them in and make them say the pledge of allegiance. They do not really believe in this and it will make them leave you alone." One afternoon the man looked out and saw a woman coming up to his door. He opened up the door, invited her in, took her into the den, stood her in front of the flag and led her in the pledge of allegiance. Then the lady said, "I've been selling Avon products for 30 years and this is the first time this has ever happened to me."

Jesus invites us to come in — to come to him. When we accept his invitation to be with him we are on the road that leads to life.

We may not have all the answers, but we know that Jesus Christ is the answer.

We may not be all we should be, but with the help of Jesus Christ we will become all we could be.

We may not always be on top of the world, but by the grace of God we will have the best of both worlds, this world and the world to come.

We may not always be right, but our lives are drawn to him who is the light.

We may sometimes lose our way, but our hands are in the hand of him who is the Way — the Truth — and the Life.

A woodsman came upon some Boy Scouts out in the wilderness. When he saw them he said, "Are you lost?" They answered, "We don't really know where we are, but we're not lost. We are with our Scoutmaster and he knows the way home."

When we are with our Master we find the way. And he invites us to be with him. Remember something else.

II

Jesus will meet you at the place where you hurt the most. Jesus met the blind man at the point of his need. He said to Bartimaeus, "What do you want me to do for you?" Jesus was asking him, "What do you need? What is the problem? Where is it that you are hurting?"

That is the question he always asks us — "What do you want me to do for you?" What is it that you really need? Is there some great hurt in your life? Is there some great burden which you bear?

Whatever it is you are not alone in your struggle. Christ invites you into his presence and there he will meet you at the place where you hurt the most.

Years ago there was a professor at Candler School of Theology at Emory University named W. A. Smart. He wrote a book called *The Contemporary Christ*. Christ is our contemporary. He comes among us and meets us. He understands us, whatever it is we are facing.

I attended a meeting of our conference board of ordained ministry where we interviewed candidates seeking to be ordained at our upcoming annual conference. One of them was a woman who had been born deaf. She told us that at the age of 15 she had an operation which enabled her to hear. Someone asked her what it was like the first time she could hear. She said, "Noisy!" She overcame the silence and the noise and met Christ in the middle of her struggle.

Has life become too noisy? Perhaps there is too much going on around you and within you. Christ will meet you in the midst of it.

A preacher was at a movie one evening. It was one of those films on the life of Christ. When the story came to the crucifixion scene the preacher noticed two young ladies in front of him. As the nails were being driven in his hands one of the girls said to the other, "Let's go, this is the place where we came in."

It always is, of course. And so often it is in the depths of our experience that Christ comes in. He meets us there. Then remember this.

III

Jesus will give you a new vision. He gave the blind man a new vision. Jesus said to Bartimaeus, "Receive your sight, your faith has made you well." Then Luke tells us that this blind man who now is able to see became a follower of Jesus. He not only received his sight; more importantly, he was given a new vision, a new vision of himself, of the world, of Jesus and how he could follow him.

Jesus Christ still opens blind eyes. He still offers to all of us a new vision. If you will accept that new vision he offers you will see things you have never seen before.

I have always loved that hymn: "Turn your eyes upon Jesus, look full in his wonderful face; And the things of earth will grow strangely dim, in the light of his glory and grace."

Some things will grow dim but some will be seen more clearly.

You will see — if you dare to look — more clearly the person God created you to become.

In a small town five men operated bakeries, all on the same street. One put up a sign, "Best Donuts in Town." So the others put up signs which said, "Best Donuts in This State" — "Best Donuts in The Country" — "Best Donuts in The World." And the last one put up a sign which said "Best Donuts on This Street." You will see a vision of your best self where you are.

You will see — if you dare to look — the best way you can follow Christ.

You will see — if you dare to look — the things about your life you need to change and the ways God is calling you to change the world.

Some see the world and say, "Look what the world is coming to." Others see Christ and say, "Look what has come to the world."

Some see things as they are and ask why. Others see things as Christ can make them and ask why not.

71

Some see only problems and give up. Others see Christ is the solution and give him their lives.

Some see nothing but shadows and spend their days living in the dark. Others see Christ the Light and live by the new vision he has given them.

Over a period of several months a man had cataracts removed from both eyes. He went back to his doctor for a final check. The doctor handed him a bottle which contained the cataracts, and said, "This is the thing which kept you from seeing." The man replied, "Doctor, I want to thank you for giving me my sight back. I want to thank you for a new set of eyes. I'm glad I don't have my old eyes. I have seen some things lately I never saw before."

Jesus will give you a new vision. You will see some things you never saw before.

When Robert Louis Stevenson was a boy he was being cared for one evening by a sitter. The sun had just gone down. Little Robert went into the living room and looked out into the darkness. As he stood there he saw a lamplighter coming up the street lighting the street lamps. And, he turned and called to the sitter, "Look, there's a man out there punching holes in the darkness!"

There is someone who will punch the darkness right out of your life. And you will see things you never saw before. And with a new vision and the light of his love you will find your way.

Pastoral Prayer

Our Heavenly Father, we gather today to sing praises to thy name and to worship thee, for thou art the source of life and from thy merciful hands we have received an abundance of good things.

Because of thy goodness we thank thee Father for blessings we sometimes take for granted, rather than with gratitude. We thank thee for sun and moon, for air we breathe, for water, beautiful flowers, smiles of children, a warm greeting, an uplifting word. We thank thee for home and family, for work to do, for energy and rest from our labors. We are thankful for the church and all it means to us. We are thankful for the fellowship of this church and the call to be disciples of Jesus Christ.

We are thankful for the way thy Son traveled the road to Jerusalem and as we think of him on that road, we pray that we would be people who would also receive new sight and new insights.

We pray Father, also, that as we offer our thanks may we also leave some other things here. May we leave any hurt feelings, pride, doubt, anger. May we leave here the desire to have our own way.

May we take from here a new resolve to seek thy will and way. May we take away from here a fresh vision, some renewed hope, more faith, a deeper kind of love.

Bless our sick and those of our church family who need thee today, maybe more than they realize.

Bless the leaders of the world with good sense and a concern for their people and all people of the world.

For we offer this our prayer in the name of Jesus Christ, our Lord and Savior. Amen.

Discussion Questions

Read Aloud: Luke 18:35-43

1. What are some things which cause us to be blind today, and rob us of a clear vision?

2. Are there ways you can identify with blind Bartimaeus?

3. How has Christ given you a new vision?

4. In what ways have you been invited into the presence of Christ?

5. At what point in your life have you been most aware that Jesus Christ has come to meet you?

6. Share the new vision you have received because of Jesus Christ and the Christian faith.

7. What has this new vision led you to do?

Closing: Have a time of sentence prayers and a benediction by the group leader.

Seeing The Light

Object: A flashlight

Good morning boys and girls. It is good to see each one of you here today. In our Scripture lesson today we will be reading about a man whose name was Bartimaeus. Have you ever heard of him? Do you know anything about him? That is right. He was a blind man.

Someone tell us what this is. That is correct. It is a flashlight. Why do we have flashlights? They help us see in the dark. If you go out for a walk at night you can use this flashlight to see where to walk so you will not fall down.

Now someone show us how to use this flashlight. That is correct. Now press the button forward. Go ahead. You did? What is wrong? I do not see any light. Can any of you see any light? Wait a minute. Something is wrong with this flashlight. Did you check to see if it has any batteries? Open up that end of it. Look inside. No batteries, no light. Oh, wait, I forgot, I have the batteries right here. Let's put them in and close it back up. Now try it. There it is. Now all of us can see the light.

There is an old song you may have heard called, "I Saw The Light." Sometime you may see in a cartoon a person who suddenly has a light bulb above his or her head. What does that mean? It means they suddenly understand something, or have an idea or see something.

In our Scripture today, Jesus gives sight to the blind man. For the first time in his life he is able to see. It is as though the light comes on for him for the first time. Not only is he able to see with his eyes, but he is able to see what his life can become because of Jesus.

Jesus helps us to be able to see. He helps us see God. He helps us see him. He helps us see ourselves. He helps us see each other. He helps us see what God wants us to do with our lives.

Jesus once said of himself, "I am the light of the world." When we see Jesus we have really seen the light and had the light turned on in our lives.

Thank you for being with us today.

May we pray: O God, keep your light shining upon us and help us to see it. May it shine on us, in us and through us. Amen.

Order Of Worship

Organ Prelude

The Lighting Of The Candles

The Choral Call To Worship

Welcome And Attendance Registration

*The Hymn Of Praise: "O For A Thousand Tongues To Sing"

*The Affirmation Of Faith: The Apostles' Creed

*The Gloria Patri

The Children's Message: "Seeing The Light"

The Pastoral Prayer

*The Hymn Of Preparation: "Come, Christians, Join To Sing"

*The Dedication Of Tithes And Offerings

The Offertory

*The Doxology

The Anthem

The Message: "The Road To Jericho" (Luke 18:35-43)

The Invitation To Christian Discipleship

*The Hymn Of Consecration: "Alas! And Did My Savior Bleed"

*The Benediction

*The Choral Response

Organ Postlude

*Congregation Standing

The Road To Jerusalem

Palm Sunday
Sermon
Pastoral Prayer
Discussion Questions
Object Lesson
Order of Worship

The Road To Jerusalem

Everybody loves a parade. I spent 10 of my growing up years in Savannah, Georgia, where my father was the pastor of a church. On March 17th of each year Savannah has the second largest St. Patrick's Day parade in the country. The whole city turns out for the parade. They dye the river green. Everybody wears green. They eat green grits. Some drink green — well, beverages. For several years I went to that parade and enjoyed watching it. But then when I was in the 10th grade I was in R.O.T.C., military training, and I marched in that parade. No longer was I a parade watcher, a bystander. I became a participant.

Everyone loves a parade. Anyone can be a bystander. It takes a little something extra to be a participant.

They gave Jesus a parade in Jerusalem — a city filled with bystanders. There were not many who were willing to participate in Jerusalem. That parade they gave Jesus was an insult.

Today is Palm Sunday and still we are haunted by those ambiguous feelings which have to do with triumph and tragedy, victory and defeat, honor and dishonor.

Today is Palm Sunday and we remember, "Hosanna in the highest. Blessed is he who comes in the name of the Lord."

Today is Palm Sunday and there's a crowd of people out there lining the street to welcome this Jesus to be King of Jews.

Today is Palm Sunday and he comes riding in on some young donkey like the old kings of Israel centuries before as they entered the Holy City.

Today is Palm Sunday and some little boy who lives out in the country is the first one to come running barefoot into town to tell us the news, "The King is coming!" Jesus is coming down the road to Jerusalem.

Today is Palm Sunday and the king is coming.

The king is coming and no one can remain neutral.

The king is coming and someone must decide.

The king is coming and you must make up your mind about him.

The king is coming and we can no longer remain the same — "something's gotta give."

Something has to change in our way of thinking.

Something has to be different about our loyalties.

Something has to be renewed about our commitment.

Something has to be chosen above all those things vying for our attention.

Palm Sunday will not let us rest, will it? It confronts us always with a choice, for always this king is coming to our city, in our place and time, for over and over again we are Jerusalem. So on this Palm Sunday, I want to remind us of what is before us today.

If we want to be bystanders — parade watchers — palm waving, flag waving Christians who go home after the parade and forget it, then we can do just that. Drop in $10, pay our dues, have a good feeling, be at ease and let the world go to hell. But, let me warn you. If you are serious about this Jesus stuff, if you want to be a participant, then you had better watch out and prepare yourself and get ready because these things are before us on this Palm Sunday. As we think about Jesus coming down the road to Jerusalem would you be aware of these things.

I

This king forces a desperate decision. That is one thing. No one can remain neutral about Jesus. We have to decide. To be neutral about Jesus is to be a "quasi-Christian."

For many Christians today church membership means no more than belonging to another civic club or fraternal order. They spend their lives in the middle of the road, the front of the bus, the back of the church, the upper level, the lower

82

profile, the outer edge of the inner group. They would rather be lukewarm than warmhearted. They would rather be contented than committed. They would rather save money than save the world. They would rather attend a Sunday brunch than a gospel feast.

On that first palm waving day, Jerusalem was full of them — those people who lived their lives in neutral gear. But we cannot live in neutral gear. No one living in neutral gear ever moved forward, or climbed a hill, or had a dream or caught a vision. There comes a time for every person to make a decision.

A boy named Gene Donaldson grew up in a little town in Texas. He was an outstanding football player. But he was having trouble deciding what college to attend. He was about ready to go to Notre Dame. Of the many football coaches who wanted him, only the coach at Kentucky went to the trouble of finding out this boy was a Catholic. That coach was Bear Bryant. He sent one of his assistants to see him and he told the assistant to dress like a priest — black suit, collar, cross around his neck. And Bear Bryant said, "I want you to tell him this, 'The Pope wants you to go to Kentucky.' " Gene Donaldson went to Kentucky and became one of Bear Bryant's first All-Americans. He made the decision.

Palm Sunday is a reminder that Jesus confronted Jerusalem with a decision. And Palm Sunday means that Jesus confronts us with that same decision today.

Some of us have a hard time deciding which crowd we want to be in — the large crowd of bystanders who watched the parade or the small crowd of participants who marched with Jesus.

Someone once asked the great Methodist evangelist Sam Jones why he came down so hard on the Methodists and why didn't he get after the Baptists. He said, "When I get through with the Methodists it's bed time."

Will Rogers once said, "Everyone wants to go to Rome to see where Saint Peter is buried, but nobody wants to live like him."

Many people would like to go to the holy land to see where Jesus lived, but so many people will not let him live in their hearts.

Almost every person in this country believes in God, but how many people really put God first in their lives?

Palm Sunday means Jesus confronts us with a choice — a desperate decision. Then something else.

II

This king requires our dedicated devotion. If we make a decision for Jesus, then we are giving him our dedicated devotion. That is what it takes to be a Christian in today's world.

It was that way from the beginning. Those 12 disciples were there with him. Jesus did not face Jerusalem alone. They were with him not as tag-a-longs, but as his loyal followers willing to face Jerusalem with him. It is true they did not understand all that was going on. It is true they would not be able to stand up under the stress of that week. They would sleep, deny, betray, hide and lose their faith. But they were there and they were devoted to Jesus. They dedicated their lives to him.

That is what Palm Sunday requires of us. It is as difficult to be a Christian today as it has ever been. The followers of Jesus have always been a minority. We are in the minority today. And there are so many things today which compete for our attention.

We are bombarded day after day with the idea that we can be happy, satisfied, forever young and beautiful and have well-adjusted children, and never have heartburn, indigestion, acne, gray hair, headaches or ring around the collar if we will just spend our money on all the right stuff. It is a lie!

We are told that our status, our value, our reputation, our worth is found in what we eat, drink, wear, drive and where we travel for fabulous vacations. It is a lie!

I think I read in the New Testament about a man who filled up his barns and then tore them down to build new ones to fill up again. Then he said to himself, "I have it made." Jesus said that man was a fool.

Jesus offers us the only alternative to the philosophy of a society gone mad over amassing things and that is a new center to our existence which puts Christ and the kingdom of God above everything else.

Jesus offered Jerusalem that choice on that first Palm waving day. That choice is before us today. We can choose to be dedicated disciples who devote all we are to Christ and the kingdom.

One Palm Sunday we had two children's choirs singing. The younger choir sang the songs, "Zacchaeus" and "The B.I.B.L.E." Then their leader said, "Now we are going to sing 'Jesus Loves Me,' " and a little three-year-old girl said, "That's my song!"

We can choose to sing the song and live the life of dedicated devotion. That choice is before us today on this Palm Sunday. Then something else.

III

This king offers a dangerous destiny. That is the third thing. If we make a decision for Jesus and give him our dedicated devotion, then we are headed for trouble.

It does not solve all our problems. It could create more. It does not make life easy. It makes some things more difficult. It does not make things simple. It makes some things more complicated. It does not bring rewards and riches. It could cost us everything. It does not assure us of anything miraculous. It leaves us to struggle with the mundane. It is dangerous to be a Christian.

Jesus had spelled out what it means — "Deny yourself, take up the cross, follow me." He had been telling the disciples all along that he was going to Jerusalem to face the cross and there would be a cross for them. As they got closer to Jerusalem, James and John came up to Jesus and asked for places of honor, on his right and on his left. He assured them they would have a place, but it would not be what they thought. They would have to drink from the same cup from which he would drink. Their destiny as disciples of Jesus was to be a dangerous one.

As Christians today, everything is not sweetness and light. We have a dangerous destiny. If we serve this king we must be willing to give ourselves, take a chance and never count the cost.

God is calling us to be his witnesses in today's world, for there is no private Christianity. He is calling us to be servants, for there is no sideline Christianity. He is calling us to be his church, for there is no uninvolved Christianity. That is before us today.

A missionary home on leave was to spend several months speaking in churches. In order to help people understand where he was serving he decided to purchase a globe of the world. He went in a store and looked at several. The clerk showed him one which had a light on the inside. And the clerk said, "Of course a lighted world costs more." The missionary answered, "Yes, I know it does. A lighted world costs everything."

Would you like to have a lighted world enough to give all you are and have, enough to join Jesus out there on the road?

When the Salvation Army first went to India, the British authorities were concerned about them, and issued an order that no open meetings and no parades were to be held. But Commissioner Tucker of the Salvation Army decided that order must be defied. One day the Salvation Army came marching down the street. They were met by soldiers. The officer in charge said, "In the name of her majesty, the Queen of England, I order you to disperse." But Tucker replied, "In the name of the King of kings, I order you to stand aside." They stood aside.

One day, one palm-waving day, Jesus marched right into Jerusalem, the Holy City, and said to everything unholy, "Stand aside." And he is calling us to join him in the parade, and to say to every form of hatred, bigotry, ignorance and apathy, "Stand aside," and when we dare to do it those things will stand aside. His kingdom will live in us, and we will help spread his rule in his world.

Would you dare to do it? Come join the parade.

Pastoral Prayer

O God, our Father, on this Palm Sunday as we come together here, enable each of us to open our hearts and lives that the king of glory would come in and may we say from the depths of our being, "Hosanna in the highest! Blessed is he who comes in the name of the Lord."

Help us to open our lives to the coming of thy Son. And during this week enable us to remember all he went through. Call us to watch and pray with him.

We thank thee, Father, for all the ways thou hast blessed us, for we have received out of thy abundance far more than we ever dreamed we would have. We have seen thy hand at work in our lives to bring about good for us, to bring hope out of struggle, peace out of suffering, strength in the midst of our struggles and the light of thy love has been shining along the path we have traveled.

Grant us, Lord, some other blessings. Give us patience with those who try ours. Help us to forgive those who would utter false evils against us. And help us love even those who are difficult to love, because they are loved by thee.

Give us always the attitude of our Lord who was always bigger and better and more brave than his enemies.

Bless our sick. Touch them as only thou canst touch them and no man can. Touch their hearts for that is the healing they need.

Give us peace in the world and help us to be peacemakers, for Jesus has said in that we will be sons and daughters of thine and we pray in the name of the Prince of Peace. Amen.

Discussion Questions

Read Aloud: Mark 11:1-10

1. Have each person share experiences related to parades.

2. Let each person share the feelings of being a part of such an event.

3. What is the meaning of Palm Sunday for you today?

4. In what ways does Jesus Christ still enter our lives?

5. What are the things which could block him and prevent that entrance?

6. What kind of decisions has Christ brought about in your own life?

7. In what ways is your devotion to him expressed?

Closing: Let each person pray for a new openness to Christ and his call in our lives, with the group leader ending with a benediction.

Welcoming The King

Object: Palm branch

Good morning boys and girls. I am so glad to see you today. This is a very special day. Do you know what today is? It is Palm Sunday. Again this year, as we do every Palm Sunday, we asked all of you to come in behind our choir waving these palm branches. Can any of you tell us why we do this? Do you want me to tell you?

When Jesus had been preaching and teaching for about three years he and the disciples went to Jerusalem for the Passover season. This was a very important Jewish holiday. They had done this before, but this time Jesus knew there were people there who wanted to kill him.

As Jesus and the disciples came into Jerusalem he rode on a donkey. For many years long before this, the Jewish kings had come into the city this same way. So Jesus was entering the city like a king. The people there welcomed him like a king also. They waved palm branches and shouted "Hosanna! Welcome to the king!"

Most of those people did not really mean that. They did not really want Jesus to be their real king. And he knew they did not want him. He knew they really wanted him to die. They wanted to kill him. Jesus knew he was going there to face the cross.

We still remember this today. This next week is called Holy Week. All during this week we will be remembering the things Jesus did during his final week. This will help us prepare for next Sunday, which is Easter Sunday.

Now, let me tell you some things to remember about Jesus the king and how we welcome him.

He is still our king today. He is the one who rules over us. So we want to love him and serve him. And we want to do all he wants us to do.

His kingdom is inside of us. We live in his kingdom, the kingdom of God. And that kingdom lives inside of us.

What does this make of us? We are people who represent him. Paul, who wrote much of the New Testament, said "We are ambassadors of Christ." We are his people wherever we go. Remember these things on this Palm Sunday. Thank you for being here.

May we pray: Father, we thank thee for Jesus, who came to be king of all the world and of our lives. Help us to always serve him. Amen.

Order Of Worship

Organ Prelude

The Lighting Of The Candles

The Choral Call To Worship

Welcome And Attendance Registration

*The Hymn Of Praise: "Lead On, O King Eternal"

*The Affirmation Of Faith: The Apostles' Creed

*The Gloria Patri

The Children's Message: "Welcoming The King"

The Pastoral Prayer

*The Hymn Of Preparation: "Hosanna, Loud Hosanna"

*The Dedication Of Tithes And Offerings

The Offertory

*The Doxology

The Anthem

The Message: "The Road To Jerusalem" (Mark 11:1-10)

The Invitation To Christian Discipleship

*The Hymn Of Consecration: "Are Ye Able"

*The Benediction

*The Choral Response

Organ Postlude

*Congregation Standing

The Road To Emmaus

Easter Sunday
Sermon
Pastoral Prayer
Discussion Questions
Object Lesson
Order of Worship

The Road To Emmaus

A man and his little grandson were out walking down the beach one afternoon. They saw a crowd of people gathered around a man who had been overcome by the heat of the sun and had suffered a sunstroke. The grandfather was trying to explain this to the boy. The little fellow looked up at his grandfather and said, "Grandpa, I hope you never suffer from a sunset."

We have gathered today to celebrate the good news that even though we face many sunsets there is always a sunrise.

There is a simple beauty in this Easter story we have read today about Jesus and two of his followers on the road to Emmaus. It shows us the great contrasts which were so much a part of that resurrection experience. Those followers of Jesus — and all who loved him — faced a sunset on that fateful Friday. The sun went down on all their hopes and dreams.

Jesus captured their imaginations, but the Roman soldiers captured him.

Jesus gained their love and devotion, but the forces of hatred divided them.

Jesus inspired the best in them, but now they have experienced the worst.

Jesus had apparently claimed a victory, but now they have seen his utter defeat.

Jesus had stood for the kingdom of God, but the power of Rome was standing over him.

Jesus had promised a better life, but is now the victim of a bitter death.

Have you ever experienced anything like this in your own life? Have there been some times when you have about lost your way? Has your life been filled with nothing but sunsets, when all you ever wanted was a little bit of sunrise? I wonder if I am speaking to someone today who has traveled a long and lonely road? If so, then Easter speaks to you.

It happened that on that first Easter day, two loyal followers of Jesus were walking down the road to Emmaus, a little village outside of Jerusalem. They were going home in defeat, shame and disappointment. It was late in the evening and the sinking sun reminded them of the sinking feeling they had on the inside. But as they walked along, a stranger joined them. He asked what they had been discussing. They stopped dead in their tracks, looked at each other and then asked him if he was the only person who did not know what had been going on for the last few days. He asked them what things were they talking about. They replied that they were talking about Jesus of Nazareth, a mighty prophet and how he had been put to death. Then they said, "But we had hoped he was the one to redeem Israel."

". . . we had hoped . . ." What a note of tragedy in those words. But it is out of that great tragedy that God brought history's greatest triumph.

Those two followers went on to relate how they had heard some of the women had found an empty tomb, and others had gone to the tomb, but did not see him. And then the stranger says, "O foolish men, and slow of heart to believe all that the prophets have spoken! Was it not necessary that Christ should suffer these things and enter into his glory?"

This is the glory of Easter, the glory of the New Testament, the glory of Christian faith, the glory of the Christian church. This is why we have gathered here on this Easter Sunday to celebrate the good news of the resurrection, because God stepped into history and said to the forces of evil, "That is enough. You can have no more of my son. I'll have the last word about this."

So, as we celebrate this today and think about the risen Christ on the road to Emmaus, would you allow your heart and mind to be filled with these things?

I

The resurrection is a transformation which takes place in our living. The resurrection changes everything. That stranger walked with them all the way home. He told them so much they wanted to hear more. They invited him to come and stay with them. They sat down at the table for a meal together. He blessed the bread and broke it. Then he gave it to them. There was something strangely familiar in all of that. And then Luke writes, "Their eyes were opened and they recognized him." Suddenly everything was different. The entire situation was transformed. Nothing would ever be the same again.

The resurrection has changed everything. Nothing is the same. Not long ago I bought a book with the title *From Upper Room To Garden Tomb*.

Instead of putting Jesus up on a throne, they put him down in a garden tomb. Those disciples had followed Jesus from up in Galilee all the way down to Jerusalem — down the streets and up to the temple — down in the garden and up to the cross — from upper room to garden tomb. And that was the end of that, they thought.

In one of our Sunday school classes a teacher was trying to help her children understand the meaning of Holy Week. When she was explaining Good Friday she said, "Now this Friday is called what? Good — Good what?" And one little boy replied, "Goodbye."

Old Pontius Pilate, the High Priest and all the members of the Sanhedrin poked each other in the ribs and said, "Goodbye. Goodbye Jesus!" And all the people who loved him hung their heads and said, "Goodbye Jesus." But their last goodbye was a new hello for Jesus went from the garden tomb around by Emmaus and back to the upper room.

Nothing has ever been the same. From that moment on, all those who followed Jesus lived in the power of his resurrection. A transformation took place in their lives.

It takes place in our living. Our living is different because we are no longer the same. We are no longer living under the power of sin and death and darkness. We live now in the light of God's love, in the dawn of a new day. Because of that the meaning of our lives has been changed, has been transformed.

In World War II a soldier was mortally wounded while fighting in Germany. He knew that the war was coming to an end, though he would not live to see the final victory. He said to a friend, "Would you give my wife a message? Would you tell her I had the joy of knowing that we have won the victory?"

Because of the resurrection of Jesus Christ, the meaning of our living has been transformed. Regardless of what might happen to us we can have the joy of knowing the victory has been won.

Then something else.

II

The resurrection is a conviction which grips our thinking. It is more than something we merely believe. It is a conviction which takes hold of us. After the risen Christ had revealed himself to those two followers he vanished from their sight. And they said to each other, "Did not our hearts burn within us when he talked with us on the road, when he opened to us the Scriptures?" They knew they had been in his presence. Their thinking was gripped by that conviction.

That is what we need today — some great convictions to live by. Like all times this is a time when we do not need any more people who merely have opinions. What is needed today are people who have great convictions.

In a church's Easter pageant there was a scene where a large cardboard box was used for the tomb. There was a boy inside the box playing the part of the angel. At one point he was to say, "He is not here. He has risen. Come see the place where he lay." But he forgot his line. Nevertheless, with all the unction he could muster, he yelled out "He ain't here. He's done gone!"

Once during a time when Martin Luther was greatly troubled, some of his friends saw him writing with his finger in the dust on a table, "He lives. He lives."

When our thinking has been gripped by that conviction, then we can face anything that comes along. When our hearts burn within us with that conviction then we know we can handle all of life.

But then something more.

III

The resurrection is a witness which inspires our sharing. It is more than a change in us, more than just a conviction. It is something we also live. It is a witness we share. Luke tells us that same hour those two followers left Emmaus and went back to Jerusalem. They went to the upper room and found the disciples. They shared what they had experienced that day. It was something they could not contain within themselves.

The early church was the result of the resurrection. Those disciples were not looking for some new organization to join — some club to which they could belong. The church was the result of their witness. The resurrection was a story they had to tell — a conviction they had to announce — a witness they had to share.

Our gathering here is a witness to the power of the resurrection. Our Christian living is a witness to the power of the resurrection. Our giving of our lives to Christ is a witness to the power of the resurrection. Our commitment to a servant church is a witness to the power of resurrection. Our love expressed in sacrificial ways is a witness to the power of resurrection. Our words of comfort and hope are a witness to the power of the resurrection.

The resurrection of Jesus Christ has made Christians out of us and our lives are a witness to the power of it. And this power continues to sustain our living. It gives us hope for today and all the tomorrows which await us.

99

On the final night of his life when the Washington preacher Peter Marshall lay dying, he said to his wife as she left his room, "I'll see you in the morning."

It sounds a lot like Jesus when he promised, "I am with you always."

He stands among us even now and promises to meet us on the roads we travel — on the highways and byways — when the sun is shining brightly — when the skies are cloudy — in the midst of all our sunsets he promises us a sunrise — "I'll see you in the morning."

That is the glory of our faith.

Eternal God, Father of our Lord Jesus Christ and great God of Easter, who has brought from the dead thy Son and our Savior, we come here to sing praises to thee and to claim for ourselves a great resurrection faith. So give us this gift of faith, O God, and enable us to be resurrection people.

Make us people, Father, who say, "Yes" to life in the face of all its contradictions, all of its "Nos" and all of its disappointments. Give us the power of the resurrection that we may live in the light no darkness can put out.

We thank thee, Father, for this good news we celebrate today and for all thy gracious blessings upon us, for thou art the source of all good things. We thank thee for life, home and families, for this church and the call to be disciples of the kingdom of God.

Forgive us when we lose our way and fall short of thy will and sin against thee. Make us to be the people thou would have us become.

Give us a vision, O God, of the world as thou would have it. No, we already have that vision. So enable us to live up to it and allow peace to break out all over the earth that thy will might be done.

For we pray in the name of our risen Lord. Amen.

Discussion Questions

Read Aloud: Luke 24:13-35

1. What is the earliest recollection you have of death?

2. Describe what Easter was like for you when you were growing up.

3. What is the significance of the things we do during our Easter celebrations?

4. Though Easter is a matter of faith, in what ways have the truths of the resurrection been proven?

5. What is the most important thing about the Easter faith to you?

6. How has this been of help to you?

7. In what ways can we share and witness to the Easter faith?

Closing: Allow each person who wishes to share a prayer, to be closed with the Lord's Prayer in unison.

The Greatest Day In The World

Object: Easter egg

Good morning boys and girls. Today is the greatest day in all history and I am so glad to see all of you here in church on this Easter Sunday.

I want to show you an Easter egg we had at our house. This egg is not very heavy. Would someone like to hold it? Be really careful with it. It is not as heavy as the ones you have at home, is it? Do you know why? I know, let's open this egg up and see what is in it, and why it is so light. Look. That egg was empty. There was not anything inside of it.

The tomb where they put the body of Jesus was empty on the first Easter morning. It was just like that egg. There was no one there.

Not only was the tomb empty, but the women who followed Jesus and the disciples all saw him and talked with him. Even though he had been put to death, he was now alive again. God had raised him up. He had overcome death.

That was the greatest day in the history of the world. Because of that day, you and I and all our loved ones may also overcome death. Jesus won a victory over death. We also have that victory and we will live with God forever.

Easter is still for us the greatest day. It is the best day for all Christians. That is why we celebrate it the ways we do.

We hide and find Easter eggs. We wear new clothes because they remind us of new life. We put on new clothes because it is our way of showing how we put on new life.

Did you know that if it were not for Easter we would not even be Christians today? We would not have this church. We would not know about Jesus. We would not have the Bible.

We would not know about God. We would not understand why we were born. We would have no hope in the face of death.

Because of Easter our lives are made better and God gives us the gift of eternal life. That is why Easter is such a great day for us. It is the greatest day in the world.

I am so glad all of you have come to be here today and that we can have this time together. I hope the rest of this day is wonderful for you and your family.

May we pray: O God, we thank you for the good news of Easter, for what it means to us and to all the world. Help us to live better because of it. Amen.

Order Of Worship

Organ Prelude

The Lighting Of The Candles

The Choral Call To Worship

Welcome And Attendance Registration

*The Hymn Of Praise: "Christ The Lord Is Risen Today"

*The Affirmation Of Faith: The Apostles' Creed

*The Gloria Patri

The Children's Message: "The Greatest Day In The World"

The Pastoral Prayer

*The Hymn Of Preparation: "Low In The Grave He Lay"

*The Dedication Of Tithes And Offerings

The Offertory

*The Doxology

The Anthem

The Message: "The Road To Emmaus" (Luke 24:13-35)

The Invitation To Christian Discipleship

*The Hymn Of Consecration: "Crown Him With Many Crowns"

*The Benediction

*The Choral Response

Organ Postlude

*Congregation Standing